Praise for Dannabang Kuwabong

Echoes from Dusty Rivers

"These moving, electric poems—for a lost family member for this precolonial, for the planet—take their strength from a never-failing belief in the power of story to reanimate and celebrate. We need this warning, this celebration, now more than ever."

—Professor Lorraine York, Dept of English,
McMaster University

"In *Echoes from Dusty Rivers*, Dannabang Kuwabong achieves a brilliant collage of re-membering of emotional, historical, cultural, and environmental voices in a move towards collective healing. Like his other two books, this collection is also a sumptuous delight of unforgettable read and re-read."

—W L (Stan) Martin, author of *Murder in Jamaica*

"*Echoes from Dusty Rivers*. It expands and deepens Dannabang Kuwabong's craft. It radiates with intellectual challenges, cultural inventiveness, stylistic surprises, and thematic diversity. *Echoes from Dusty Rivers* mediates on human issues cross-culturally with a richness of spirit to celebrate personal and collective pain and hope. *Echoes from Dusty Rivers* is a universal work; devastating war against the environment . . . the loss of our roots in the land, displacement, and confusion are deeply familiar. Our longing for a life in harmony with nature and each other sings out here, loud and strong, with great beauty."

—Professor Anne Savage, Dept of English,
McMaster University

Voices from Kibuli Country

"A powerful, incantatory work within the praise song tradition that limns locality, the local and the specific—from Hamilton, Ontario, to St Croix, West Indies; from the urban landscape of North America to the lush, verdant environment of the Caribbean. Kuwabong carefully and lovingly incises his poetry of place on the palimpsest of lost memory. His words summon long-forgotten ancestors who have never left us and draw a circle around the many disparate voices of Africa and the Afrospora. *Voices from Kibuli Country* is here, is there, is everywhere where the pain of exile exists."

—M NourbeSe Philip, author of *She Tries Her Tongue,*
Her Silence Softly Breaks

"An archipelagic adventurer, Dannabang Kuwabong arrives in the second decade of the new century from seemingly random shores, sighing, singing, certain, with a poetic text of assiduous import."

—Lasana M Sekou, author of *The Salt Reaper: poems from the flats*

"These poems, lush, sharp, pliable and aromatic, are about love that one finds in a place and among a people, Haiti, St Croix, Dominica and elsewhere in the Caribbean. Each poem invites you to enter, rest and reflect for a while . . . A cohesive collection with great surprises."

—Opal Palmer Adisa, author of *Eros Muse* and *I Name Me Name*

sargasso sea scrolls

poetry

DANNABANG KUWABONG

MAWEN*Z*I
HOUSE

We acknowledge the support of the Canada Council for the Arts for our publishing program. We also acknowledge support from the Government of Ontario through the Ontario Arts Council, and the support of the Government of Canada through the Canada Book Fund.

ONTARIO ARTS COUNCIL
CONSEIL DES ARTS DE L'ONTARIO
an Ontario government agency
un organisme du gouvernement de l'Ontario

Canada Council   Conseil des arts
for the Arts   du Canada

Canadä

Cover design by Sabrina Pignataro
Cover image: Mesut Ugurlu/Deep underwater ocean scene stock photo/ iStockphoto

Library and Archives Canada Cataloguing in Publication

Title: Sargasso Sea scrolls : poetry / Dannabang Kuwabong.

Names: Kuwabong, Dannabang, 1955- author.

Identifiers: Canadiana (print) 20230230326 | Canadiana (ebook) 20230230334 | ISBN 9781774150979 (softcover) | ISBN 9781774150986 (EPUB) | ISBN 9781774150993 (PDF)

Subjects: LCGFT: Poetry.

Classification: LCC PS8571.U89 S27 2023 | DDC C811/.54—dc23

Printed and bound in Canada by Coach House Printing

Mawenzi House Publishers Ltd.
39 Woburn Avenue (B)
Toronto, Ontario M5M 1K5
Canada
www.mawenzihouse.com

In loving memory of my late uncle,
Most Reverend Gregory Eebodong Kpiebaya (1933-2022),
Archbishop Emeritus of Tamale, Ghana

Contents

Hurricane Meditations

Less I Forget: Reflections of a Run-away Father

Not a Preface

Sargasso Sea Scrolls is an unfinished work of the imagination. The landscapes are real. Each poem arises from a vision in a particular Caribbean space from which ghosts appear from memory to confront the seer and interpreter of dreams, the poet. The title came to me aboard a yacht after the 12th conference titled "Islands-in-Between: Language, Literature, and Culture of the Eastern Caribbean," held annually and held that year (2009) from 5 to 7 November in the Commonwealth of Dominica. Following that conference, a well-to-do patron invited participants to take a short trip to the Sargasso Sea and have dinner aboard his yacht. I hardly expected that I would be seeing the same endless seascape that my African ancestors from Northern Ghana saw as they were taken from Elmina Castle on the Coast of Ghana to Roseau sugar plantations. The Sargasso Sea is full of rotting algae and "bounded on the west by the Gulf Stream, on the north by the North Atlantic Current, on the east by the Canary Current, and on the south by the North Atlantic Equatorial Current," creating a secure and mysterious watery deep with unrevealed histories. [https://en.wikipedia.org/wiki/Sargasso_Sea]

As I sat on the deck waiting forever for food, I began to understand why the Sargasso Sea is called a "dead [watery] zone," with its concentric currents that seem to take the seafarer nowhere. And here I was alone among a crowd that understood their watery surroundings. I had no foothold in the Caribbean but saw my face in the faces that claimed me as an ancestor without knowing me. I, a nomad from Northern Ghana, on a personal odyssey of discovery to various Caribbean islands, have been obsessed with looking for lost ancestors in rocky caves, volcanic sand beaches, smoky mountains, flat landscapes, abandoned sugar factories, and aging great houses. Most of all, I sought to sniff out the ghosts at the grave-yards, where the echoes of my ancestors' voices may still echo in their bleached bones below the waters. Then, a vision. A hand rises up from the depths of the Sargasso, brushing off dead plastic algae from a pot with leopard designs, signaling my clan. I reach out and receive the jar. Then the breeze blows. The yacht moves. Dinner finally arrives. I am not hungry. We sail back to land. The Sargasso Sea Scrolls are reminiscent of the biblical scrolls that were hidden in a cave in Egypt and are called the Dead Sea Scrolls.

In this collection, the voices narrating the individual and collective histories of my translocated ancestors clarify and justify my odyssey from Ghana through Canada to the Caribbean. The poetry shows the Dagaaba slaves to be keen observers of Caribbean landscapes and interpreters of historical memories, and it explains the connections between West Africa, Europe, and the Americas. It records the anxieties that the slaves absorbed from the sea and the foreign land and culture and the comforts they found.

Divided into six sections, each poem in *Sargasso Sea Scrolls* evinces the poet's refreshing encounters, haunting visions, a celebratory discovery, and discoveries of nostalgic gems in Aruba, Costa Rica, St Eustatius, Curaçao, St Thomas, Puerto Rico, USA, and Canada. The Scrolls together draw attention to the perennial natural disasters in these archipelagoes, which are often described as Islas del Encantos, and they question whether the disasters result from human misbehaviour. The poems articulate in raw language the human suffering described in my *Caribbean Blues and Love's Genealogy*, *Voices from Kibuli Country*, and *Echoes from Dusty Rivers*. Each poem is a narrative, a medallion of suffering and a testimony of resistance and survival. The collection is a concentric gathering of voices that establish the connection between the histories of the Dagaaba and other peoples from Northern Ghana, who may have formed the larger population of the enslaved, that are often buried in the swirling narratives that privilege slave empires in West Africa.

In this work, each experience is different yet linked to others across island spaces. The reader will be surprised by every image, symbol, word, paragraph, and poem. *Sargasso Sea Scrolls*, as an archaeological treasure trove, answers the call for writers from the continent of Africa to participate in the pan-African ideal of trans-Atlantic crossings. It stresses the important point that the search for African roots cannot rest only with the diasporic African looking to Africa.

Ritual Potsherds Beneath the Sargasso

Libations of Remembrance

                    from above
dark   dustless   desert
hugs shiftless sea clots of clouds
        white fear   rain
            manage no mirages of hope
                slug   forest reserves a little you
                    gesticulate   challenge the curios eye
                    the sea sees the sleepy
                    monsters muck around swirls
                        dark blue deeps i cannot tell you my friend
                    Mami   Wata   shampoos
                        flings locks traps breezes
                        shakes out tornadoes typhoons hurricanes
                        thunder lightening for landing rights
                        on this rock treelorn rock?
somehow someone survived
                        crop-over in sea-belly
                                sweaty-blood blending
        sea-water
        life

Libations of Remembrance

(All around.   blue emptiness.   then Aruba.)
The poem a libation
obelisk for sleepers
below these constant waves
pushing   Aruba and Ghana!
   Denu sea   hugs this dark flat stone
thorn bushes and cacti
shifting bridge   between   Mpalaba   Aruba
trepidation   my foothold   tripping violent waves
Below left-over crags   hollow reefs   broken borders
Gatherings from distant lands reassemble
Tell of other arrivants   on this land   look aside.
allure in tourist brochures,
chips off molten Eden's granite
now salt altars and bowl of waterless rain
ritual tools to revoke
Africarawakan nightmares
Hissing volcanoes our cell memories
clangs toward "great houses" of pain.
build your imitation altar
seven square translucent stones
offer unremembered penitence
without memory only concealed blood
these pleasure shores.
oblation: dried crab cases.   Stir beneath Atlantic mists
rainbows dazzling below rocks
bleached bones rhyme and rhythm.
against artificial mastiffs
or mini-altars jogging along coastline.

dreams similar clumps of earth stone angels
watchful sentries at windows of no returns
MAGNIFICENT WHITE SHADOWS
block coastline of Ghana,
companions of lost memories
trick toys kidnap erasable memory
unregister spirits riding moaning sea waves
looking for homeplaces.

Eating Kadushi

She
bullies us with tales of fossil rocks
yaps about black rocks
holes that breathe lives
Aruba sprang
like a squat giant
from a troubled sea
sighs the last gasps
of Arawaks and Dagaaba slaves
those stroked the waters
between Curaçao and Surinam
cling behind *Watapanas*
monsoons whipping them toward sunsets
memories hidden at cross-seas
where sunrise paths rise to origins.
Eat *kadushi*
drink *bringa mosa* bush medicines,
Eat *kadushi*
without *kobi* or *dawadawa*?
Eat *kadushi*
whisper their names
on these *yatu* with the lips of *seida*
Eat *kadushi*
carve ritual circles on faces
of these *ayo* rocks
mushroom termite mounts rise at *Falingtan*
claim my childhood at *Falingtan*
mushroom hills of Nanvilli
we play again hide-and-seek

under the sombrero shades of the hills
calves and kids do mock battles
careen practice courtship
then I see faces
scripted in *Quadiriki* Caves
mourning rituals to ward off despair
the days of massacres,
secret curses for bibbers of misery
at *Bushiribana* mines,
flying litter chokes Arikok National Park
ruins of piracy now
pirate cove for ruffling Benjamin Franklins
the Juliannas, Maximas, and Elizabeths too
For now, it is Queen Maxima of Holland,
roused sudden searches for lost jewels
among neglected backyards.

Counting Potsherds

I dip my torn foot
in the sea-salt of history
pay homage to souls
dragged from Gwolu   to Salaga's unction blocks
snatched from Sankana caves   to Edina or Oguaa yard sales
I remap my three Voltas   for hope
                    slippery
only death by drowning   lacerated against whipping trees.
          visionary of dying
     I resist the verdant of peace at Baby Beach
Ghanaian Dutch sisters seek empowerment
Billboards of dreams departures   Billboards of arrivals
Aruba   ◀━━━━━▶   Jirapa
those who seek reinternment in Sankana Caves
we who seek forgetting in *Quadiriki* Caves
I alone swim in the still waters in the Cavernas del Río Camuy in
    an Isla del Encanto
Seeking   *Muuli-Nye-Kono* (Peek-See-
    Wail)   at Duong
I scarify my palms with signposts   depart for Puerto Rico
At Miami Airport   I miss Nanvilli
This poem shall be my libation to remember
                    those who sleep
                    below the waves
    riding potsherds scattered over uncertain landscapes
                    Statia and other seascapes!

(Freedom F(L)ight) Yuastajes (aka Statia)

Conquistadores frigates tug
at these rugged moorings.
Sails shake off blue and green wind strokes.

Pink roofs of gabled storied houses
hide bloody histories
starless vacuous azures   stretch into silence
dormant volcano without men-of war bounce against these waves
somnambulating obmutescent mountain shadows
irritate umbilical fears and strangle my conticent euphoria
then silhouettes of shadows strip around me
screaming, lacerating, wiss-swirling, with shimmering noon heat
my skin cringes. tightens. quivers. steel-ready against whip's
    shearing
curling for the prodding, punching, poking, kicking
in twelve plantations on Saladoid ground

Mister Moore reclines surveys his Golden Rock
sucks hard at fresh-bone pipe from Arouac shins
inhale perfumes from composting cadavers in wrestling dugouts
mapped by bleached skeletons as memory
at the raise of his withering hand
a voice decrees:
from Statia to Bonaire, Curaçao to Aruba, and Sint Marteen
"be ye all informed to take note:
A negro wench, by name Nonche
A mulatto bloke, by name Johny Donker
A Congo woman by name Candice
All for re-capture or for sale at ƒ4."
I beat back blistering emotions

Arrest unbridled mind wait
Thomas Dupersoy I hear is strolling by
Leading that hopeful and faithful fifty
Through slippery stony paths
To Quill Volcano   to freedom
Johannes de Veer   fumbles   among his askaris
A bloodied saber will never cut them down
What remains are ruins
Quilting spaces for new legends
Amisiereh, I whisper to Misha Spanner, griot and guide, thank you
Keeper of memories of my people
Promises meant to keep at my going.

Night Shift

Avoiding the stern tower of the Seventh Day Adventist Cathedral
boondocking in hallowed shadows of Congo Reserve
We crouch around hurricane lamps with fired expectations
Maybe this is how our ancestors must have felt
We required no recognition codes but in spirit
As Brother Joshua, memory keeper and pointer
Recounts forgotten encounters of struggle
Recounts half-hushed myths of victories
Of those who like us rose from ships' bellies
Marched barefoot and raw knuckles
To snatch freedom from iron bangles
And sticks that thundered and murdered
Brother Joshua, keeper of word secrets
Tells us in hushed tones of reverence
"at this very spot below the Quill, below the Quill
Yet unremembered in Statian narrative brochures
Or labeled among sites for nickel chinking tourists
Just so the future may not reflect the past"
I quip in the anxiety of my apprehension:
"Perhaps the desire to erase
Is a balm to pain of re-membering"?
"Yes," Brother Magumbo calms my trepidation
"Memory can be scary if carelessly unleashed
It breaks old scars into new bloody wounds
Disintegrates new promises with old betrayals."
We squat around for a reasoning and a groundation

Meditation in da Deep Yard

unhinged stones of broken dreams   imported addictions and
Garvey's dreams droop   shrivel.
a vision. a passion. that somber day.   Screams against
consumption's slavery
clangs of Dupersoy's fisted breaks of visible chains
Still echoes in the tower bell.   de Veers ghost shivers and
whimpers
veering to deny Dupersoy's secured freedom in volcano vaults.
Sucks at his knighthood cloth broiled in African blood.   I stoop. i
select. three broken bricks
Dream a fire place as altar to sacrifice.   Silence.
Make fillet of word sound.   Where? at Looli and Concordia
Black Harry whistles *sankeys* as welcome blues
adorn my humbug-up at Godet and Zeelandia.
       I scramble to Mansion and Glass Bottle
       nothing but re-visioning tales
         I trail to Behind and hear the *booby*'s
         lament
           How *couvalli* and the *mesple* are
           foregone
             the *macamba* no more to behold
Suddenly. She rushes up to me. Is my trance?
Drapes my sweaty neck   with a shimmering of rosaries. Sparkling
blue beads
Singing songs of overcoming
           Recalls nos oficios de la memoria to
           Puerto Limon.

Oficios de la Memoria: Puerto Limón

Puerto Limón.
I recall your gentle embrace
Hoy.   exito.
We crawl toward San José
                    Everywhere mountains.
Misty mastiffs
Hedge uncertain gorges
Behind smoke integuments
Offerings to drowsing volcanoes
Distances beyond measure
Between earth's forever kisses
Memory a slug   squirming   to scorched beginnings.
Ahora, yo se de tormento
Soundless expressions
Corrupted in empty costumbres
Se delinearon nuestras identidades
Tangled tunnels of exilio espiritual
Without plastron for retreat
From our desplazamientos, we
Peel through scabs of violence, we
Glimpse flashes of nuestros sueños.
So, for you my love, I recall Puerto Limón
Abierta la puerta de nuestos renacimientos
Edulcorate these sleazy fragments of our pain
Pounding breasts of Caribbean islets
Firing silent violence of history
You keepers of hope's recipes
Spark delicate hymns of our heritage
Exorcizar los duendes malos

13

En nuetros duelos de plantaciones
Burn and restore this yearning
Recover ambitions planted
Here in Liberty Hall
Where Garvey's lone voice
Rose above ruination
By these rivers of despair
Ignite re-membrane's fire
Cuddle seascapes and landscapes
Receive lost myths lodged in griots' throats
Absent lullabies as children's songs.
Poetic hairstyles birth new horizons
Unveil eloquent ghosts of stories
In deft illusionistas of multi-culturalismes
Reject this disting of our scars
As we seek only our redefinitions balms
Reveal the healing power of our visions
In theaters of memory
In this tierra dificil
Perform our presencia
Our spirits will rise at Manzanillo
As nature's spectres above despair
Dance toward los centros de todos los recuerdos
These bamboulas in el teatro de nuetras Memorias
Are las metamórforsis de nuestros recuerdos in Bomba City.

Bomba City

Bomba City
wobbling water over swollen swamps
bridge between an impatient sea
distant mountains of Limon
lean on squat shacks
sudden raring of rusty roofs
sautéed and broiled
puffing salty vapors rise ghostly
glide toward a tired sea under a hostile
sun.

Bomba

Counterpoint
twirls of relations
shadows interlocking shadows
arms convulse against sweaty thighs
twitch tricked by drummer's call
Unheard are ghostly laughter
Screeching sounds
ska in rocksteady against reggae
kaiso rides mento to zouk
only the bamboula rises in company
gathers waves like skirts across oceans
claim rhythms of relation
in transplanted half-steps, hesitant
behind inside-out soles like duendes on Rio Banano banks

Rio Banano

a shimmering.
a frothing green moss.
slimy streams gathering
moving toward sleepy Puerta Limon
then:
        inflate Rio Pacuare Rafters
        splash mud-bathing crocs
        then Rio Tarcoles and Rio Celeste.

Rio Celeste

Shimmeringly!
Resplendently!
open blue mouth
thirsty for divine water
filtered in volcanic rocks.
thundering vapors
call out ghosts of Dagaaba
to seek watery ways back home
westward to death
eastward to life.
Say. In your blue stillness
do you meditate upon rhythms of your flow
sort soul pilgrims from stomach tourists
trickle out mystery waters
to lap their way Leeward
in the gyrating swirls of the Sargasso
to sandy sunrises
shores of sea memories?
or squat   lost in sloth sanctuaries?

Sloth Envy

2:00 post meridian past siesta sleep
sloths curl up in their *hamakas*
heads covered by fat hairy arms
exhaustion after Caesar salad breaks
of leafy greens, crunchy twigs, bursting buds, bugs
we with no desire for rest
tire emotions to wake you
we try baby coocoo chatter
we beg for a wink in our selfies
we berate you for your self-indulgence
feel slighted in our entitlement to pleasure.
at last, nightmares of being barbecued at human fiesta,
a baby sloth groans, lazily lifts an eyelid
unexciting scene
yawns, and powerful yellow molars
then again spread-eagles on her back
farts into a snore. we scream the Ew! Childlike!
disperse enraged bandanas masking nostrils.
a baby sloth squeals in delight. farts some more.
Rio Vizcaya beckons.

Rio Vizcaya

Sleepy brown water
Sprawled over soft spongy banks
Makes a twisted crawl
To the Estero Negro
Beside expanding banks
A rickety jet begins a shaky dance
Twin granny engines come to life
Dodge reckless gendarmes of teak
Misses *Sixaola* of Talamanca
Wind-swipes *Hotel Playa Westfalias*
Dashes drunkenly
Staggers forwardly
Lurches here and lurches there
Aiming at cavernous cracks
Then. Miracle.
It squeaks. It groans. Lifts toward *Cerro de la Muerte*.
Below we view the Rio Hone.

Rio Hone

Chiquita* controls the flow of glistering waters flowing to feed
thirsty GMO bananas. prickly pineapples stand. like helmeted
sentries. row. upon row. upon row! green desert and misty suns.
a touristscope of addiction. a greedy need. I hunger only for
hoopoe† calls now.
To the three Santas:
Cibuqueira (aka St Cruz)
Aburakeiru (aka St Thomas)
Malliagonkieru (aka St John)
Dance again under starless skies
night of the silent drums
march Buddhoe from Christiansted to Frederiksted
shout Ahi-Ai and shout Ayay
raise the flag of liberation against Von Scholten.
Now I sigh for maroon daughters rise to action
Fire-burning on Queen Mary's Highway
count my days under a fake castle of Blue Bird
A touristscope of addiction in Aburakeiru
Swathed in nickels.

---

* The Swiss Company, Chiquita Brands International Inc that controls most of
the banana production in Costa Rica.
† The African Hoopoe is a cavity nester (in tree holes, either natural or made by
barbets or woodpeckers) or will happily use a hollow in a pile of boulders or cavities
in buildings, always chosen and protected by the male.

Touristscope of St Thomas

s   t   r   e   t   c   h   e   d
across bunker beds in damp Bunker Hill Hotel
wedged
between broken bricks and peeling walls that lime the rows of 103
  steps
under numbered as 99
i pant up each one one at time
i count them all

                                         one at a time
careful not to misstep in mystery of thirsty heat
under shadows of fireburn queens

Fire-burning Queens

under scattered shadows invented Black Beard's castle
fire burning Nannys of Santa Cruz rise to confront me
Queen Mary and dem:* Mary, Mathilda, Agnes, Josephine
i remember them all: one by one by name alone
these had scorched a way to a second call to freedom:
here is Agnes with a yellow duku
leading a determined charge
torch in left hand, machete in her right
to her eastern flank strides Gertrude
on her graying head a purple duku
an oil lamp to inflame the breeze
to the south rises a Matilda
a Kano cloth as her duku
her flaming torch defies the watery winds
Matilda and Gertrude hitch-up aprons
free their wombs of deadly silence
to the north appears the queen of hearts
Mary with a smoking pipe between gritted teeth
chanting:
Gangan Mimi takes us over
makes our spirits restless
until her voice is heard
down the treacle road of Babylon
so we light up these canfields
so we mash up this un-freedom
for our slippery men snigger and retreat!

---

* Reference to Richard A Schrader's play, *1878, Queen Mary and Dem* (1998).
Kingshill, VI: Richard A Schrader, Sr.

i mistake Blue Beard's castle for Black Beard's*
erected over bones of murdered wife of Frenchy
erected to cast doubts over uprising maroon daughter
conceal Viking sons' treacheries
against Mary's people by these pirate coves.
shadows rise jingling chains or change I do not know
bulging wallets of colored paper
bearing heads of distant queens and kings I know.
In sweat and tears.   Not in nickels.   Not in dimes.   Not in
    pennies.
Not in sold stories.   Not a treacle to sweeten our drudgery.
your concrete statuettes an unction plaza
to weave tourist yarns for a nickel and a half-penny
to us who would escape the cold blights of *Boreas*†
for a blast in these sunbaked sands lining the quiet sea
sprouting water-locked rocks: St Thomas; St John; St Croix.

---

*   These are two castles reputed to have been the hideouts of two famous pirates,
Blue Beard and Black Beard. Though the castle said to be Blue Beard's is disputed.
†   Greek purple winged god of the winter.

Re-counting the Steps

i wonder whose crosses are being born by the new-natives
who like the apostle will call someone his lord and his god
or like the beloved John, under whose cross the people stand?
what I hear is these male-virgins were named for guilt
that memories of certain murders in history may be erased
along with the names that they whispered before Colón
the comfort they gave Taínos; Caribs; Arawaks; Calinagos*
who in turn revered, loved, nurtured and celebrated them
in rituals of dance, song, art, without ownership claims
but walking up these 103 minus 4 steps facing Black Beard's castle
nothing else remains of that memory except façades erected
to placate the desire of those who come to stare without faith
at these invented ruins of pillage and blanched narratives
under the shadows of foreign beards not of vigilant damsels
driven mad and violent under weights of their black cargo
as they slithered and twisted down slippery mountain sides
tumbling often to uncertain graves where cruise ships dock
to empty seekers of sweet treacle from theses archipelagoes
i rearrange my own scattered beard of multi-colors
fix firmly my borrowed scull-cap to hide my anxiety of loss
stride toward Black Beard's Castle or is it to Blue Beard's
what I know now is a desired dialogue with history
                    but under the fierce gaze of my queens
i retrace my steps
                    tumble over over-littered pathways
                                        behind Bunker Hill†
                    seeking refuge among the new nobility

---

*   Indigenous pre-Columbian peoples of the Caribbean.
†   A three-star hotel in St Thomas, USVI.

carousing at Black Beard's Castle
outdoor with pageantry fresh neophytes formed
in the fifty-year cauldron of parroted indoctrination
and I, stranded on these wind tussled islands
must dip my tongue in heavy metal broth
among high-rise tombs where fresh souls seep out of broken
  ground

Metal Broth

Heavy Metal Broth at Negro Hills[*]

Sister you steam
in these cauldrons of cane
yet rise like history's ghosts
You memorialize heartbeats
in these heavy cauldrons
disturb clanging metal broths
You bottle our ancient moans
pour them out as libations of hope
and dissolve our cataract visions
You stir waters caught in hollow trunk
of the tree of forgetting[†]
we circle counter clocking
nine for men seven for women
sixteen for children of the marches
wash away Lethean mud of amnesia
return the host of remembering
Your silent gasps are the quarry
At the gates to our catacombs
Where new flares of visions light
Where your words are slivers of calm
Slithering and skittering
Above a shimmering Atlantic
Raise up bleached bones of men un-mourned

---

[*] For Asyla Holt, a poet friend of Curaçao. Her book *Enliven Emotions: Thoughtful Inspirations from Caribbean Sea* inspired some of the poems.

[†] A symbolic 'tree', known as the 'tree of forgetfulness'. It is said that the captured Africans were forced to walk around it multiple times (9 for males, / for females), so they would become dizzy and disoriented—in a sense 'forgetting' who they were for a bit and making it much easier for the tradespeople and slave-owners to 're-program' them to being more compliant and less individual.

Raise up bleached bones of women un-mourned
Those who gave their all to death
That we might sing resurrection songs
These *Kasena luse**
Across these jagged sides of Negro Hills.

---

* In Nakong and other Kasena towns, particular styles of drumming and singing that were used to rally the people during slave raids and dirges are still used today (Kasena Luse) to accompany the corpse of a member of the community who dies away from home.

Maroon Sirens

Here evenings reveal stone diaries
thornbushes fortify savannas
yet waves whitewash my bones
on ever-receding corals
as maroon flutes pierce the air
recall *bumbulla* sirens of Nakong*
men on rooftops let fly our arrows
scare away those hungry to sell us
under the baobab at Salaga†
under this baobab at Paga‡
and here, under this 800-year-old kapok at Barber§
guide my hairs of our regrets
untie me from hardened hearts
guide me through hollowed crooked trees
and rocky moss-smoothed gateways
to Fantasy forest¶ where am awaited
my flesh sprawls at Gwolu or is it Ulo** again

---

* A short flute (bumbulla) was used to draw attention to the presence of slave raiders and to rally men to fight in the town of Nakong, Upper East Region of Ghana.
† A Gonja town in the Savanna Region of Ghana where a famous slave market was erected to sell captives from as far away as Mali to Ashanti slave merchants.
‡ A well-know Kasena town in the Upper East Region at the Ghana border with Burkına Faso with a slave market in the nineteenth century.
§ The oldest tree in Curaçao at Baber on Curaçao.
¶ A place in Curaçao.
** Towns in Upper West Region of Ghana where the people erected border walls against slave raiders and successfully resisted the Zabarama and Mande slave raiders.

Sojourner

lost sojourner gazing at your shadow
in these approaching heaps of dreams
green glows of hope
red glows of pain
i share nostalgia not amnesia
a millipede i waddle in serendipity
among silent gazers of eyeless skulls
below Queen Juliana Bridge
a katolic with stumps of memory
trumps from Punda to Otrabanda
trumps past Graf Maria Magdealena
or call it Santana Berg Altena
its parade of Afro-Catholic ghosts
claim a hearing among unheard moans
feeling footfall toward home
i join with no knowledge of my going
home

Home

home then sister
is this page of memory
a tongue with anguish
begins the struggle for words
hidden in these volcanic vaults
hungry ghost stories/history
my landfall of healing soils
the whiffs of ancient smoke
invites me to these distant homesteads
shut out in Willemstad's night frenzy
direct my steps home to Popu Guayaba
or misstep and drown my way to Popu Elmina?

High Rise Tombs Diaries[*]

Epithets on Storied Tombs

"semper den nos kurason"
"Drumi dushi Big Mom"
"Rust zacht,"
others etch the desires of the left behind
fumes of sudden flesh beneath ground
seethe through new soil monuments
sail to the surface to escape the rot
seek a nostril for refreshing rebirth
i pack my Ghana Must Go bag
hasten to step away from the silent home
saunter toward tunes of heavy metal broth
my heavy metal dreaming
guide me home in tongues
i step into memory's forest
following the sound: *drumi dushi* dream walker
drumi dush dream weaver dream.

Drumi Dushi*

Saturday
dawn morning
    silence slouches   empty streets
    strange vapors   out or into hollows
i cannot tell
but trust me
trust also tomb diaries
and wait
beside B&B La Creole/Hostel La Creole
beside the market square of Willemstad.
Sephardics rest at Beit Haim Berg Altena
their silences carved
in skulls, crossbones, hourglasses
                    stone angels guard tomb stones
                    my name refuses my gaze
                I may be lucky in Roodeweg
                catacombs

---

* Sweet Dreams in Papiamentu.

Roodeweg Catacombs

                                                                 I circle back to Roodeweg Cemetery

Tiptoe around lean on tombstones
Read memories' memories
hurriedly scripted
peeling paint   yawning graves
each seek cacti history
protest europa's cavernous tastes
the honorable bloodletting

                                            my name refuses my gaze.

Kolebra Bèrdè

      intrigued
Kolebra Bèrdè
      amazed
Kas Chikitu,
      ghost hostel of unbelievers lean
i enter bursting   with expectation
i search   trepidation

Kolebra Bèrdè
Kas Chikitu ghost hostel unbelievers   rest
enter   expectation
search   trepidation
sink concealed graves yawn

Marasa Imani[*]

foreskins
of we (un)circumcised
shrivel by holy walls
await *mai kaciya*[†] at sunrise
await *mai kaciya* at sunset
before entombment
Caquetíos[‡], Africans, Asians, Moors, Katolics[§]
Above unnamed grave words:
        Drumi Dushi
        Big Mama
Below   half-exposed a face
Half-covered a headkerchief
palms interlock   tired thighs
planted   before a large cauldron
kadushi froths purifier for children
cleanser   poison of history
scattered yellow papers
kas di pali marshi.

---

* Hausa for unbelievers.
† Hausa word for one who circumcises.
‡ Indigenous peoples of Curaçao, Aruba, Bonaire at the time of European intervention.
§ Papiamentu for Catholic.

Museo Kas Di Pali Marshi

Daughter of Dong-Puong-Yeh
Below breeze-caressed *watapana** shades
Welcomes droopy-eye sojourners
With juices from *kadushi* fruits
Refreshes our parched bodies
Your wizened smiles spread
Reveal mysteries behind hieroglyphics
Carefully etched in skin parchments
Your tortured silence of look behind

I see: no we all see. I lie?
A *kadushi* sentinel sports a goat's skull
As a rooster spruces its black tail
Opens its panoply wings under a tamarind
Struts, beats a chest of many scars
Crows oft told victories combats
At annual brotherhood of the spurs games
To pleasure envious men against clans of combs

Daughter of Dong-Puong-Yeh
You stamped these word in my mind:
"burn sage wood for sanctification"
It leavens memory's dough
Bread of memory rises at sunrise
Beside history's dormant oven

---

* Native plant of the Curaçao, Aruba, Bonaire etc, and South America.

These soil heaps like one at Sandema* or Jentilpe
and moans:
"These graveyard pits of divi divi
Burnt to produce coal for braziers
For night fires when the slaves
Tired from salt mining
Returned to their hearths for stone soups

Drown ash of cactus in jars of clay
Coat ancient grain against wolfish weevils
This here foxtail millet or sorghum
These here passels of pearl millet
This here the finger millet brand."
Heat chases dribbles of sweat down brow
She stops beckons me to take over if I dare.
I need not daring
Tankama† is my praise name
I step into the silent expectation
Call each grain by its Dagaare name
The *gberi*, the *zia*, the *nabili-nyema*‡
I rattle off a few more names and smile
Call each fox or finger millet by its praise name
Trace their routes to my Sahelian roots
I stop. I behold. A shadow at the doorway
My mother's face or is it Maria of Kòrsou§

---

* In both Sandema capital of Builsa of Upper East Region and Jentilpe, capital of
the Vagla of Savannah Region of Ghana, there are gravel monuments that com-
memorate the people's collective memory of resistance to slave raids in the nine-
teenth century. The landscape of Curaçao is similar to the landscape of these parts
of Ghana. Some food crops are also similar.
† Show off.
‡ Sorghum, pearl millet, white sorghum or calf-teeth.
§ Maria of Curaçao led the Slave Revolt of 1716.

Rises like a mist of love
glides above *divi divi*
Sighs southwestward with the winds.
We exit to sip *kadushi* tea.

Kadushi

This island is not a mere graveyard
Of shipwrecks, ruins, and pirate coves
Someone chastises a dosing scholar
This land
She sings: is home to *kadushi*
Drink *kadushi* juice to purify dirty minds
Use *kadushi* juice to wash your masks
Spray *kadushi* starch to renew clothes
Lather with *kadushi* soap to shampoo hair
Make *kadushi* soup to feed the poor
In days of draught and despair
When patience cooks even stones
Pasenta ta kushiño Piedra
Pasenta ta kushiño kadushi
For guinea worm swellings
Wrap roasted *kadushi* around the swellings
Boil "pun pun kora" with *kadushi* flowers
Bathe the swollen foot at dawn and dusk
Kadushi sweetness intoxicates the worm
To death
Here sip *kadushi* juice for recovery.

Negro Hills

Besides these banks de'armor
We sit down empty-eyed
Prepare to sing our Psalm 137
Orphan songs of remembrance
Beside Barbara's homestead
As we nurture our amnesia
Refinery fumes numb my Atlantic longing
I pine like pines for eastern coasts of slaves
Ghost ships of slaves groan ghost captives
Bop their way to these islands of slaves
I snigger at ghost daughters of plantation madams
They parade my mothers' *geles** of pain
Claim and enchain my protest song to cane
I stand unperturbed
Sojourner from eastern shores
Pose with luminous smiles
Take unerasable picture
I think: I carry no burdened spirits
Somnambulating among tombs
Arabs, Dagaaba, Jews, Dutch
Dream violent history's silence
No footnote tear
For those that roamed these plains
Before the hanging at Boca Tabla

---

* Cloth head-tie worn by African women.

Boca Tabla

Three table mounts
Fly the *kinikini*
Kenib stones rise
Reveal brick hovels
Dagaaba died there
Their graves consumed
By bibbers of dark tourism
Horror dreamers scratching limbo spaces
Sponge thorns scrape skins
Pierce empty spaces
Along winding roads
Lead weary feet to Dokstertein
A white mansion rises to challenge
The squat cottage of Barbara.
A distant te deum rings from a chapel tower.

Te Deum

Under the shade of a *katolic* church
Curaçao's god is sunset on the cross
See! churches face sunsets
Here plantation lords chanted in unison
If you listen carefully yo may hear
Performed ad tedium *Te Deums* to cruelty
Testimony of their god spread-eagled on screws
To certify Arawak blood as fit sacrifice
To sanctify Dagaaba on this rock
Tula's ghost cools off with mango smoothie
And I sip singing waters from the Blue Room Cave
Before Tula's ghost* blows a conch for freedom again
Now heard only in Hato Caves by Playa Gandhi?

---

* Tula organized and led a month long slave revolt in Curaçao in 1795. The revolt failed and he was executed by the Dutch by crucifixion. He is now the national hero of Curaçao.

Singing Waters

Here by Playa Gandhi
Singing water caress coral coves
Swirl and heal broken bodies
Hiss and heal confused spirits
Blue-salt clarifying pools
Coral mists absorb pain and pang
Filter trauma toxins from bone and flesh
Filter trauma toxins from mind and foot
Deep belly-bottom yawning with health
This place for tsunami waters has becomes spas

We pass several Playas without interest
Though Kola Museum called out
We zoom past them too soon bored
No *kenapas* lined the Playa Kenapa
Only fourteen concrete fists line the road
Recall Tula's black panther spirit
1795 against *verhaals* of conquests
I stared out the bus window
Who was Abao with a Playa for his memory:
a leaning coconut tree of Curaçao?

Pund Caballero

pines are sky thieves
they lean leeward against west winds
and like *divi-divi* bend like bows
trace memory charts as pathways
to those who with no direction
on their homeward bound to Ghana

Julianadorp Rotunda

Beside Julianadorp Rotunda a ghost watches
I am/was Domingo Africanus
Man-man cross-dressed to kill
Mistaken as another desirable maid.

I am anxious for a glimpse of my sister
Clamped in massa's rape chamber
His scent eluded mongrel sniffers
night after night with tobacco-soaked steaks
I eluded those *dogo Cubanos**
nightfall after nightfall
I rub negro peppers on my skin
Drive wolfhounds to tear at their young

Nightfall after nightfall
I jiggle fake behinds at sentinels
Shyly fake a promise soon
Sneak pass knowing a misstep
Would be a dangling from a tamarind
That night I forgot my pepper protection
Two white fleece *Cú Faoil*† sniff me out
Launch their massive muscles at me
Canines glint like ancient sacrifice daggers
Miss my ankles but rip my pants
I forget stick-fighting moves
Forget kalinda dance counter strikes
i leap unguided land among white thorn bushes
three signal lightings and conch calls they say

---

* Specially bred Cuban dogs to hunt runaway slaves.
† The Irish name for the Irish Wolfhound.

three flaming torches guide my feet they say
through slippery rocks to hanging caves they say
Lit my way to protection among Maria's troops
Maria of Curaçao
Green cacti with palms outstretched
Rise like an obelisk through granite
Black thorns laced together stand guard
I beg forgiveness for my treachery
That cause our erasure in rebellion stories
Remembered to us by Amun[*] and Huracan[†]
Now I sit alone sealed in my baño.[‡]

awaiting Irma and Maria.

---

[*] Egyptian God of storms.
[†] Indigenous Caribbean and South American God of storms.
[‡] Bathroom.

Hurricane Meditations

Whooping with Irma and Maria

Prologue: I (A)

I Am. alone. I Am. sealed in a baño.   I am safe from the howl of
   history
I crank open the steel shutter
Peek.
I am enthralled more than thrilled
Maria's ghoulish screams
Drives sentries of trees to dances of death
along these haughty avenidas universidades
In these Jardins de Universidad.
But here, each tree dances, twirls
Each tree dances, leaps, waves
Each tree dances, bows, prays
Each tree dances, twists, hisses
Each tree dances, groans, whoops
Each tree dances, cracks, crashes
To Maria's conch calls to death
The tornado roars
Pummels nature dancers to penitence
For not bowing to Irma.
For not readying for Maria
Empty of grace, whooshing in wrath.

Prologue I (B)

Maria's furies   are   elegant
Converge   belligerent
                    Convert
Us into nature's zombies   our passing despair
Queue in dismay   seek new testimonies
Fill ripped forms of woe   patch scattered memories
Maria's tomahawks of furies
Swirled through her sky thieves
Circle our message towers
Crush them into ruins
And we desperate lords
Strum around with bruises
Delusional
Pray that somehow our tears
Will warm the cold hearts
Of those who decide our fates
Behind smudges of painted words
Maria's furious furies
Hammer, shatter, enshrines our uncertainties
Leave   behind   coded   contingencies   of   doubt.

Prologue I (C)

Irma, hot after Harvey's* love
Sighed, roamed disheveled
Puffed in flippant disdain
Over competing islands
puffed last breaths of power
raked through maroon sanctuaries
exposing Shango's thunder rituals
Silence sits in Pinoñes mangroves
Feisty Bomba drums sit dumb
No scratching rhythms by la guira
                              Las tamboras refuse finger carresses
The ritual fiestas de Santiago Apóstol
Los niños, los hombres y las Damas
Have lost the power to protect
As hooves trample imagined Moor's skull
Yemoja gathers her river skirt and calls Oshun
Ride waves back to Oyo to confer with Obatala
and we, we in segregated barracoons
without memory
chuckle behind *puerta blindadas*
counting Ave Marias on blue beads
kissing brass medals crossing ourselves
While between San Cristobel and El Moro
The powerful Santa Barbara wields a sword
Against any broadcast about a lost Loiza
or a pillaged Piñonez pinned to the ground
by irate Irma jealous of her successor!
Hurricane Maria. Madre de Ciclónes
Maria. Madre de Ciclónes.
La Virgen Llorona with no tears for her children.

---

* Hurricane that hit Texas and Louisiana in August 2017.

She came screaming
She came howling
whipped trees
Snapped, broke, dragged
beat them down alleys

Maria spread her massive arms
Maria flared her massive nostrils

> Maria screamed against
> genealogies of wind
> genealogies of water births
> genealogies of debt. Birthed.

Desolation its name.

Salsa Con Maria

I too would have loved to salsa with Maria
But was held captive by Irma's panic
So there I was chained ankle deep
In a porcelain tub of water
filled to forestall a future
If this forced death dance of wind and water
Would burst these ancient PEX lines
And leave me stranded
with rumbling bowels.

So, I stood, pinned to my baño window
Desperate moth drawn to suicide beams
Yet Maria steps up Irma's moves
Whistled warrior songs and danced
Flamenco-ed mahoganies to the concrete
Flung flame trees to the ground.

Slowly all others are carried along
Along the cry of drowned *culebróns**,
In this flood without an Arc of tomorrow
Mi neva si dis kaynd wata weh jam wit wind
the signpost points downward and reads:
"Mangled Against Resurrection In Anger,"
suddenly, at the crossroads to hope
a sniggering emperor draped in despair
Grins. Squints. Slam-dunks Bounty Selects
you wipe away your shock tears
stampede for Charmin Ultra

---

* Species of the boa found only in Puerto Rico.

now you stare at the dry toilet tank of hope.
There are no more rainbows of faith
only the whimper of a song scratches the windpipe
and you crumble in a pool of gurgling:
♫♫♫♫♫♪♪♪♪♪♫♫♫♫♫♫♫♫♫♪♪♪♪
And then the crash of falling trees
The flying glass
silence in a pool.

Typhoonomics

zealous effundis
traced her twirling turns
mapping, revising, mapping
their wands of knowing
held aloft in vain as if
      To push bash back
      Her bursts of breath
      As she skated bulbous waves
      Across the Middle Passage
      Echoing the moans of those drowned:
listeners, prophets, visionaries, seers, hearers, learners, critics, Eco
mechanics, magicians, saints, sinners, gurus, pundits, *marabouts*,
*karimugri**, dreamers, escapists, naturalists, atheists, storm
bibbers, and all who hold the wands of unknowing truths, to
greet dawn mist before the sun strode across a darkened blue to
streak it weakening light against a raging darkness.
                                      They all gathered.
Crowding
the doors of whirlpool oracles
the doors of whirlwind oracles
Confounded.
The faithful abandoned
Panic and rampage
Hug things as talismans
Against these days foretold
By auguries of rising sighs   across roaring sea ripples
Then, the whispers of despair

---

* *Marabouts* and *Karimugri* refer to the same persons: holy men of Islam,
Qur'anic teachers, etc in Ghana.

Rustles from leaf to leaf
Old trees like Ents* confer
Fearing a future without them
For no more bird song or coqui call
Are heard below the adventitious sign:
      A moaning of trunks and stems
      A heaving and a howling
      A wild waving of hoary branches
      A crack! A crash! A crunch.
Holed-up
      In sanctuaries of fear
Her ensigns call
these disturbing hoops of whoops
Trouble the still anxious air
Heated above perspiration
Among huddled stragglers
And we dare not stir nor stare
then you burst forth
wind volcanoes from remembered oceans
whipped to flying gallop
by defiant Mami Watas†
to trample in rage over these Virgins of Islands

then they fling their watery assegais
piercing, tearing, collapsing, crushing, scattering
all that dare defy their march to fame
and the Uwaifo's‡ song
to "never never run away,"
when you emerge from deep dripping seas
no longer guarantees our faith.

---

* *Lord of the Rings: The Two Towers.*
† Female Water Spirit.
‡ Nigerian highlife musician of the 1950s-1990s. Knighted for his cultural con-
tributions.

But,
                    Surprised at your nakedness
                    You grasp these salted waters
                    Your wrappers of defiance
As you slouch, dance, rush, forward
Glean Dominica, St Martin, Antigua, Barbuda, the Santos of
    USVI,
and boot-dance like deep earth miners
empty water lodged in boots
over every hill and valley

stripping trees of their leaves
you scythe your path through plantain farms
peeling bananas green and yellow
limes and avocados your slingshot stones
as mud balls crash through glass gates
slashing and drowning
                    all those who dared to stir
then exhausted and disillusioned
you gasped like and ghost and faded
and we, now orphaned
crawl out of our cloaks of panic
to map what is left of our inherited dreams
        and the effundis
                    cluster
                            chins in palms
                                                wondering
why we wander so much.

Maria Ciclónes 1

Maria Ciclónes.
We hail your name.
We wept and weep
At your advent
Recall the terror of Hugo
Whom some rename
Hell Under God's Orders
For after Irma's glancing slash
At Piñones and sand-duned Loiza
We who squat above glass ceilings
Giggled, nervous with hope
That perhaps this was all
For a pardon may be a re-wind
As we keel to kneel
Drugged by novenas to Joe
And sprinkled invocations of the lamb's blood
Across our doorways that crossed Maria's pathways
We scrawled five rosaries of Ave Marias
Then we sat.
then we waited.
Then we hoped.
T h e n w e p a n i c k e d . !
As wind-chasers mapped
Your rushing footfalls, Oh Maria:
In every which watery ways
Cast doubts in certain ways
That your foot aim
May yet un-target us

Then
bamkurudududududududu
and!
Covid-19 gurgles
ripples across masses of flesh

.

Maria Ciclónes 2

Maria Ciclónes. We prayed.
Let your coming be a blessing
Ameena.
Then despair spread across the land
Silence. Steamy silence. Silence. Irate silence.
An approaching shadow
Covers the quivering sky
Covers homesteads with terrible history
Through the centers
Of these Islas del Encantos*
These dream escapes for those coming in from the cold
Sifting ricos from their puertos
Then we wonder and wander
Like new nomads from the middle passage
Castaways, newly branded for sale
To those who would pay with abuse
And so we cry:
Oh Maria Ciclónes
We will erect an obelisk
An obelisk of memory
As we re-member our trumped memories.

---

* Islands of enchantment.

Maria Ciclónes 3

In these arcadias on Calle Las Marias
Lining competing oceans
The Sargasso boils
The Caribbean swirls
Puke the raging winds into the Atlantic
Puke against strips of this Isla del Encanto
Where snickering promises
Smirk through sniggering airways.

I have waited for this fulfilment
confirmed prophecy at my doorstep
as nature's forces swoop down
Whooping winds role water
As cannon balls, hurl them
Crashing and tearing our strongholds
Others stand sentry, block all exits
With barriers of uprooted Fabaceae.

This then is what the ancients foresaw
That nature's ritual dances of death
Take back in swift flashes of power
What we desire and desecrate
Think we control and own

Then we hug a dance of wind and water

We inhale the stench of nightmares in our souls
But soon forget only to recall
At the whisper of winds between
New eaves under a darkening sky
The appointed time of Passover is here!

Passover

After the Passover of Irma and Maria
On these Virgin and enchanted isles
We were spared death's glances:
In our hallucination we
Saw nothing, recognized nothing
Touched nothing against our nakedness
Promised nothing on land, air, or sea
Only the sun smiled, blazed, burnt, set
Only the stars strutted, twinkled and shut
Air wet like steamed baths hung low
We gasped and questioned dream escapades
of those with no history of Huracan's anger
with drooping heads, we wandered dazed
We turned and we turned, trudged into ruined castles
We spun and we spun, jumped under blankets of fear
Wondered: is this how the children of Isis felt
When the angel of Yahweh stumped their sons to death?
For Maria and Irma must be soucouyants
Who sought the spilled blood of Osiris's.
Isis scouts the Mosquito Bay in tears for those unsung.

Maria: Madre de Ciclónes

you awaken on the day of Maria's rage
meet your nightmares strolling
through these Islas del Encantos,
these ravaged paradisos
where las touristas seek escape
to dream of abundant ecstasies

today you cringe, startled
locked inside your hotel toilet
afraid of the roars of competing winds
of the wrath of boiling seas
no one to transfer your fear of winds

sheared leaves and broken branches
unveiled roots, shattered trunks
strewn, mangled, twisted, tangled
gather in heaps like garbage

paradise sprawls, dry-eyed
licks a lacerated body
across new gullies slashed
by disorderly waters chasing
after unruly mud zombies
they slide, wriggle, roll
drunk unsteady boulders
down these ancient valleys
amuse your Maria of nightmares
you bite your quivering lips
your fingers bloodied on rosary beads
you chant litanies of saints

in still squeals of supplication
you recall a hymn you long repressed
after that confirmation tap by the bishop
on that Feast day of Maria's Assumption
♪♪♪♪♪♪♪♪♪♪♪♪♪♪♪♪♪♪♪♪♪♪♪♪♪♪♪
Hail, Queen of heav'n, the ocean star!
Guide of the wand'rer here below!
Thrown on life's surge, we claim thy care;
save us from peril and from woe. [. . .]

Only Maria's bawling answers
you are a sucker for airwave promises
you await the count of losses
for words, for feeling, for faith
confirmed in your surrounding:
and you belong no more.

you recall only how that night
how Maria's panyaring raids
on these Islas del Encantos
began a new way of dating
you recall the whooping of Shu
the pounding of Huracan's anger
to now revision your search
through these concrete walls
plant your toe-prints gently over
these sprawling fabaceae
their supplications yield no pardons
you meditate on your minuteness

this is what the ancients foresaw
that nature's ritual dances of life
take back in swift flashes of power

what you worship as normal
think you control, can modify, own
but now you stand dismayed
in this place of virtual pleasure
a soul's shadow in coming days
trembling your fear in tenor:
Sojourners in this vale of tears,
To thee, blest advocate, we cry.
Oh, pity our sorrows, calm our fears.
And soothe with hope our misery.
Refuge in grief, Star of the sea,
Pray for the mourner, Oh, pray for me.

you wonder whether your sins
brought Maria's vengeance
on these raped Virgin Islands
to make them paradises of forgetting
you arouse the jealous rage of Guabancex*
in her eternal fertility dance with Amun†
and West Africa meets the West Indies
you are transfixed in horror and awe
listening to the dance of spheres

---

* Taíno goddess of the wind.
† Ancient Egyptian god of the sun and wind.

Maria: Madre de Ciclónes: Revision

you dreamed to bomba with Irma
you dreamt to merengue with Maria
you dreamed to salsa with Shu*
in the days of Huracan's awakening

yet at the appointed beat
your feet refuse to rise in step
the nightmares of Irma's passing
freeze your wrinkled heart
you stand now soaked
in this swelling of waters
swirl, wash pasts into futures
when Quebui† blows his ram horns
gathers hot winds of a cancerous tropic
gather Capricorn's steams from Huracan
and there is no present in your standing

you are pinned to the baño window
behind those hurricane shutters
a desperate moth quivering
you wonder at Maria's majesty
you cannot escape the call of fear
Maria steps up Irma's moves
blows her bullhorn blues
waltzes and trips haughty trees
to over-bend, crack, crash
uproot concrete pavement.
the winds rake through your head

---

* Egyptian god of the wind.
† Egyptian god of the north wind.

carry snatches of drowned voices
toward a new Gethsemane or Golgotha
the signpost points downward and reads:
"Mangled Against Resurrection In Anger,"
suddenly, at the crossroads to hope
a sniggering emperor draped in despair
Grins. Squints. Slam-dunks Bounty Selects
you wipe away your shock tears
stampede for Charmin Ultra
now you stare at the dry toilet tank of hope.
There are no more rainbows of faith
only the whimper of a song scratches the windpipe
and you crumble in a pool of gurgling:

                                  crash. shattering glass. silence.
What is left but birthday confessions

Less I Forget: Reflections of a Run-away Father

Hallucinations of Defeat

I fear no one cares whether I live or . . .!
three score years have caught up with me
donning scattered shadows of my youthful dreams
scattering sludges of despair all around
to mock the jetsams of my atrabilious faith
my hope an apprehended darkness

I turn ecliptic or epileptic
Can't recall. count remnant flickers
un-re-member my slivered heart
mind pummeled by regret's paroxysm
Oscillates toward nanoseconds beyond repair

hearthrobs detonate to mummification
love's cruel fluids curdle in its tributaries
Putrefy in the harsh commas of hesitated love

I glimpse the screens of past pathways: All vanity!
"The labor that I labored to accomplish
wrung wrongs my hands wrought
fooled foolishness fixed as wisdom
in this land I sing as home and native land?
Where the spectacles to my grandstands?
What pageants for the vexation of my heart?"
This sardonic debenture of nullity?
A lingering life ravaged in crepuscules
As I hide in the gulley of Black Creek
tribulations guard my mausoleum
abrogate any straying memorials
scatter passing whispers of my name

in these icy hours to my cessation

name the fame maculed in this lacuuna
of memory chips of those I craved for
my morrow brought nothing but sorrow
and sprinkled over melting snow
these spots of fleety vacuity
viral divinities rule my termination
on these snowy capes at flat mountain
Ratify nothing at Water Front
Only a crumbling monument of moss
Erected to amnesia: I am unmarked. unmasked

for i fear no one really cares whether i live or . . . !

Tired of Me?

"I am the man . . . [forgotten]"
(Lamentations 3:1-2)

How come my heart wanders
shamed in solitude's regrets
Its solitary rhythms uncertain
That formerly fussed in anticipation
Danced to multitudes of laughter
Now a schlep in desolation
No comforting grin from passers-by.

Yet.

Those who would lasso my angst
cut hasty retreats at Niagara Falls
thunderous claps of laughing water
distract as mist swallows my frame
I hurtle down the rocky slopes
My geronimo shout dovetailing
the thunder of the Falls

I float. I drift. I dip down below.
Cloaked in gall gown of untriumph
Over the big O of my zeroings.
My words shatter.   My breath scatters.   The water hisses.   In
disgust.

——

Dejection becomes my new name
Praise names limp away refuse adulation
there are no tributaries for an overflow into
these tired arteries and they collapse
Unspoken is my vernacular of tenderness

Turn riot into a turbulence of cacophony
Lips reddish purple from winter words
Wrench sapplings of whispered allegiance
From wounded hearts of tortured minds.

                                        Yet.

I strive to sing with the sea gulls
I strive to scream with he dolphins
of filtered desires that await somewhere
I try to sigh and whistle like winter winds
Slaking warm dewlets from pine trees
unable to escape the role in snow storms
With no cave to hide my fear of coming darkness
I ask only forgiveness for my rumination.
Of a man forsaken. howling behind the living. Howling at the
   wind at moontide.

Tears at Lolipop Loop

Here in Lolipop Loop
I dream forgiveness.

Lost in Lolipop Loop
I whom am children blessed
I anoint you in my head
I bless you in my heart
I know you as my body
But,
Somewhere in my turbulent emotions
I must seek your mercies and forgiveness:
Forgiveness for absconding
Forgiveness for unfeeling
The meanness with understanding
Miserliness of encouragement

Here in Lolipop Loop
I dream forgiveness.

Forgiveness for forever Atlantic crossings
In search of enchanted glories
In search of dreams escapes
I made you take charge of my crises
I failed you though I gave bribes of oreos
A cancer of mental flumoxity
That now rise up like zombies of uncharted futures.

Here in Lolipop Loop
I dream forgiveness.

Yes. unashamed I offer praises.
Your chests of courage
Are monuments of light
Shining through despair's darkness

At Tew's Falls in Dundas Peak
The sacrificed dreams that guided the startled boat
Across these many turbulent years
Charted your paths without my shadow.

Here in Lolipop Loop
I dream forgiveness.

I beg forgiveness
for so much
rolled into a single cry:
If you could find clean throbbing hearts,
If you find empty spaces in your minds
If you find forgiveness in your spirits
grant forgiveness.

Belated Rumbling Thank Yous

On this day when both sun and cloud competed
I determined to burst through my birthwaters
Cried for love and attention from a tired mother
Dragged my indigo cloth begging to be carried
On the burdened back of a drooping mother
As she sowed millet under unrelenting suns
And all the nights I woke her up for milk treats
From teats made sore with playful gum bites
And the many times I caused strife and bitterness
Between her and other mothers in the compound
                                    Yet she never stopped loving me
                            Yet I never got to thank her at my growth
For she passed from daylight into darknight
Now I thank her for not leaving me unloved
She sent one with equal depth of love
To nurture and see me grow and thrive
She too deserves all my unalloyed gratitude
Mothers, I am the boy who never knew his way around
Yet walked off the village square in pride
To seek and to find what he did not know
                    Thank you my two mothers: Bolale and Gyiinama
                        Your love, hope, and faith in me helped me grow
This is just to thank you father
Your fierce unyielding faith in God
Sowed a seed in me to trust God
Your disciplined kindness that welcomed all
Trained me to show a smile to everyone
And to empathize with those who travail
You saw my faults through our difficult years

Yet you always believed in me beyond myself
Helped me cast aside my dark self-doubts
To raise me to the potential best I could be
I wish to thank you for so many other things
That showed me what and how a father should be
Though I did fail you in many ways
                    Thank you Kuwabong though you are gone
                    Your love, hope, and faith in me helped me grow
Daughter of Galyuoni and Angbanangyeleh
You rescued me with your sterling love and patience
A man whose world whirled and tossed with uncertainty
You came up with healing words and hopeful dreams
You humbled yourself to lift and prop a lowly man
You made no demands in recompence or despair
But only to journey with you to Kingdom come
Your prayers began the journey in Canada of your dream
                                        Thank you
                            Your love showed me the way
I have not always been grateful
Tried to cancel your faith with doubts
drove you to beyond despair
yet you never wavered in your vision
I cannot ever thank you enough

                                        Thank you
                            Your love showed me the way
                        You have been my reference point
                    No joy without your selfless embrace
Thank you though you are gone   Your love is not in vain*
                    1843 or 2003?

_____

* So ends the salvageable portions of the Sargasso Sea Scrolls discovered by an
itinerant seafarer lost on the black sand beaches somewhere in the Grenadines after
Hurricane Maria in 2017. A lot of the scrolls got burnt by La Grande Soufrière vol-
cano eruption in 1843 in Guadeloupe. Others got damaged by hurricane winds. All
errors in the manuscript are the original writer's not the editor's or copy editor's.

Acknowledgments

My first thanks go to my family, whose love and support provide the light to see my way. I offer praise to the Dagaaba praise and dirge singers, storytellers, xylophonists, flutists, and drummers and, most of all, to the grandmothers and aunts who often fired up my imagination with weird midnight stories of dancing corpses, complaining dead bodies, disappearing waters, etc. They trained me to hear the chuckles and groans, see what was confusing or certain, and feel the memories of silent landscapes wherever I went. I thank Nurjehan Aziz and MG Vassanji of Mawenzi House Publishers for their constant encouragement and readiness to publish and promote my work. Without their unflinching support, my other books, *Caribbean Blues & Love's Genealogy* and *Voices from Kibuli Country* might still be gathering dust or water in a dark box. Thanks go to my friend, H Nigel Thomas, for his constant support and edits to some of the poems. Thanks also go to Opal Palmer Adisa, Lasana M Sekou, Nickolas Faraclas, Martin Egblewogbe, Anne Storch, and Shujah Reiph, whose encouragement means a lot to me. I must remember the gathering of poets in Curaçao and Saint Eustatius, who provided me the space to read some of the poems in this volume at their poetry slam nights. To the University of Puerto Rico, and the University of Curaçao that funded my trips to the various islands to attend conferences and out of which the poems were born, I say thank you. I am most of all grateful to the Canada Council for the Arts/Conseil des Arts du Canada and Ontario Arts Council/Conseil des Arts de L'Ontario.

Some of these poems have appeared in literary magazines such as *Kola: a black literary magazine; Eleven Eleven; The Mouth: Critical Studies on Language, Culture and Society; The Caribbean Writer; The Prairie Schooner; Sargasso: A Journal of Caribbean Literature, Language, & Culture; Interviewing the Caribbean;* etc.

Dannabang Kuwabong is a Ghanaian Canadian born in Nanville in the Upper West Region of Ghana. He was educated in Ghana, Scotland, and Canada, and teaches Caribbean literature at the University of Puerto Rico, San Juan. His publications include *Konga and other Dagaaba Folktales; Visions of Venom; Caribbean Blues & Love's Genealogy; Echoes from Dusty Rivers;* and *Voices from Kibuli Country.* He lives in Hamilton, Ontario.